Beethoven : The story of a little boy who was forced to practice

by Tapper, Thomas, 1864-1958

ISBN: 9781318988266

Copyright © 2016 by HardPress

HardPress
8345 NW 66TH ST #2561
MIAMI FL 33166-2626
USA
Email: info@hardpress.net

Ordering Information:

Quantity sales. Special discounts are available on quantity purchases by corporations, associations, and others. For details, contact the publisher by email at the address above.

Printed in the United States of America, United Kingdom and Australia

Directions for Binding

Enclosed in this envelope is the cord and the needle with which to bind this book. Start in from the outside as shown on the diagram here. Pass the needle and thread through the center of the book, leaving an end extend outside, then through to the outside, about 2 inches from the center; then from the outside to inside 2 inches from the center at the other end of the book, bringing the thread finally again through the center, and tie the two ends in a knot, one each side of the cord on the outside.

THEO. PRESSER CO., Pub's., Phila., Pa.

HOW TO USE THIS BOOK

THIS book is one of a series known as the CHILD'S OWN BOOK OF GREAT MUSICIANS, written by Thomas Tapper, author of "Pictures from the Lives of the Great Composers for Children," "Music Talks with Children," "First Studies in Music Biography," and others.

The sheet of illustrations included herewith is to be cut apart by the child, and each illustration is to be inserted in its proper place throughout the book, pasted in the space containing the same number as will be found under each picture on the sheet. It is not necessary to cover the entire back of a picture with paste. Put it only on the corners and place neatly within the lines you will find printed around each space. Use photographic paste, if possible.

After this play-work is completed there will be found at the back of the book blank pages upon which the child is to write his own story of the great musician, based upon the facts and questions found on the previous pages.

The book is then to be sewed by the child through the center with the cord found in the enclosed envelope. The book thus becomes the child's own book.

This series will be found not only to furnish a pleasing and interesting task for the children, but will teach them the main facts with regard to the life of each of the great musicians—an educational feature worth while.

This series of the Child's Own Book of Great Musicians includes at present a book on each of the following:

Bach

Grieg

Mozart

Beethoven	Handel	Nevin
Brahms	Haydn	Schubert
Schumann	Chopin	Liszt

Dvořák

Foster

MacDowell

Mendelssohn

Tschaikowsky

Verdi

Wagner

BEETHOVEN
The Story of a Little Boy Who Was Forced to Practice

This Book was made by

Philadelphia
Theodore Presser Co.
1712 Chestnut Str.

COPYRIGHT, 1917, BY THEODORE PRESSER CO.
British Copyright Secured
Printed in U. S. A.

BORN

DIED

[Pg 3]
The Story of a Little Boy who was Forced to Practice

Ludwig van Beethoven was born in the lovely town of Bonn, on the River Rhine, December 16, 1770. The house in which he spent his boyhood is still standing. We see in the picture what a pretty, homelike place the house and the yard must have been. It is now the Beethoven House, or Museum, filled with mementos of the great composer. There you may see music pages written by him, letters, medals, instruments; even his ear trumpet is there.

THE BEETHOVEN HOUSE

Beethoven's father was a singer at the Chapel of the Elector. He was not a good father, for he did not care to work even enough to make his family comfortable. But the mother loved her boy with all her heart, as we shall see.

BEETHOVEN'S FATHER

Ludwig was only four years old when he began to study music. Like children of to-day he shed [Pg 4] many a tear over the first lessons. In the beginning his father taught him piano and violin, and forced him to practice. At school he learned, just as we do to-day, reading, writing, arithmetic, and later on, Latin.

THE FIRST LESSON

Never again after thirteen, did Ludwig go to school for he had to work and earn his living.

Do you wonder what kind of a boy he was?

We are told that he was shy and quiet. He talked little and took no interest in the games that his boy and girl companions played.

While Ludwig was in school he played at a concert for the first time. He was then eight years old. Two years later he had composed quite a number of pieces. One of these was printed. It was called *Variations on Dressler's March*. On the title page of this piece it said:—

> VARIATIONS ON
> DRESSLER'S MARCH
> Composed by a Young Amateur
> LOUIS VAN BEETHOVEN
> Aged ten years. 1780

[Pg 5] Then the little boy studied with a teacher named Christian Gottlob Neefe, who took real interest in him. Neefe did not, as was said of Beethoven's father, punish the little boy severely to keep him at his practice, hour after hour.

Often when Neefe had to travel Ludwig took his teacher's place as organist at the Court. Then with the organ lessons there were other lessons in Harmony. So rapidly did the boy improve that his teacher said one day:

"If he goes on as he has begun, he will some day be a second Mozart."

Our young hero of thirteen was surely busy every hour of the day. He played in an orchestra, as accompanist. He gave lessons, played the organ in church, studied the violin, and kept up his work in composition. He always kept a note-book for musical ideas.

Most every child in these days has more and better opportunities than had the great Beethoven when he was a child. Here is a picture of the funny old organ in the Minorite Church of Bonn upon which Beethoven played when he was a little boy.

BEETHOVEN'S ORGAN

Look at the funny stops at the top and compare it with the best organ in your own town. This is little better than a toy beside [Pg 6] our fine organs of to-day,—yet it was the best that Beethoven had to practice upon. When Neefe said that he would probably be a second Mozart the words filled Ludwig with a great desire. On his sixteenth birthday what do you think happened? Why, he set out from Bonn to Vienna, where Mozart lived.

But scarcely had he begun to feel at home in Vienna when news came to him that his mother was ill. She had always been a good mother, kind of heart, great of hope for her little boy, and probably she sympathized with the hard lot that made him have to work so early in life. When he learned of her sickness he hastened to Bonn.

Who was happier, he said to one of his friends, than I, so long as I was able to speak the sweet name of Mother and know that she heard me?

BEETHOVEN'S MOTHER

Vienna had given him a wonderful happiness. He met Mozart and had some lessons from him in composition. When he played for the great master, Mozart tip-toed from the room and said softly to those present:

[Pg 7] "Pay heed to this boy. He will surely make a noise in the world some day."

BEETHOVEN AND MOZART

After his Mother's death he determined that he would remain there. And it was not until he talked with Joseph Haydn, who stopped at Bonn on his way to London, that he decided once more to journey to Vienna.

Beethoven was twenty-two years old at the time he met Papa Haydn. Beethoven showed the master some of his compositions. Haydn urged him to go at once to Vienna, promising to give him lessons in composition on his return from London.

JOSEPH HAYDN

[Pg 8] Everywhere in Vienna Beethoven was a welcome guest. He was proud (but in the right way), very honest, always straightforward and independent.

But, like his mother, he was warm-hearted and as true as could be. There was nothing in his nature that was mean, or cruel, or wrong in any way. He took pride in his talent and worked hard to perfect himself in it.

Here is what Beethoven's handwriting looked like.

BEETHOVEN'S HANDWRITING Listen

Bit by bit, the great power of Beethoven as a pianist became known. He played much among his friends, but he did not like to perform in public.

A story is told that once he was to play his C major Concerto at a concert. When he arrived at the hall he found the piano was tuned so low that he had to play the Concerto in C# major.

You know how hard it is to transpose a simple piece, but think of transposing a Concerto and playing it with orchestra without time for practice!

Do you sometimes wonder what the great composer looked like? Beethoven lived outside of Vienna and often took long walks in the country. Once a little boy ten years of age was taken by his father to visit Beethoven. The boy must have been a very observant [Pg 9] boy for he wrote out a description of how Beethoven looked. This is the little boy's picture as a man:

CARL CZERNY

And this is the description he gave of Beethoven.

"Beethoven was dressed in a dark gray jacket and trousers of some long-haired material, which reminded me of the description of Robinson Crusoe I had just been reading. The jet-black hair stood upright on his head. A beard, unshaven for several days, made still darker his naturally swarthy face. I noticed also, with a child's quick perception, that he had cotton wool which seemed to have been dipped in some yellow fluid in both ears. His hands were covered with hair, and the fingers were very broad, especially at the tips."

You know, of course, that when we think of music we think of *hearing* it. We think how it *sounds* to us. A lover of music loves to hear its *tones* and to feel its *rhythm*.

Like every other human being, Beethoven loved music in just this way. He loved its sounds as they fell on the ear. As colors delight our eyes, so tones fell with delight upon the ears of this man.

[Pg 10]Beethoven was once invited to play at the home of a nobleman, but upon being informed that he would be expected to go as a menial, he indignantly rejected the proposal.

THE ANGRY BEETHOVEN

Beethoven had many friends and was fond of them. They knew that he was a genius and were glad to forget some of the very strange things that he did when he got angry. Here is a picture of the great master seated among a group of his friends. Although Beethoven was odd, his friends loved him.

BEETHOVEN PLAYING FOR HIS FRIENDS

[Pg 11] But a strange Fate touched him and took away his sense of hearing. From the time he was about thirty years old his hearing grew gradually worse. Indeed it was necessary for him to have a piano especially constructed with additional wires so that he could hear.

BEETHOVEN'S PIANO

Can you think of anything more cruel, more terrible, more depressing, more awful?

BEETHOVEN IN THE COUNTRY

[Pg 12] And yet he went on day, after day, composing beautiful music as he walked the fields, or as he sat at his table. For we must remember that he could hear his own music in his thoughts. That is, the mind that made the music could hear it, though the ear itself was forever closed to the sound of it.

Year after year he continued to write symphonies and concertos, sonatas, songs, choral and chamber music.

And year after year the poor ears closed a little more and still a little more, until finally not even the loudest noises could penetrate them.

And yet he worked bravely; writing every beautiful music thought that came to him, so that the world, and that means you and all of us, might have them. When Beethoven was dying in 1827, Schubert called upon him and remained with him for some time.

BEETHOVEN AND SCHUBERT

[Pg 13] SOME FACTS ABOUT BEETHOVEN

Read these facts about Ludwig van Beethoven and try to write his story out of them, using your own words.

When your story is finished ask your mother or your teacher to read it. When you have made it as perfect as you can, copy it on pages 15 and 16.

1. The composer's full name was Ludwig van Beethoven.
2. He was born at Bonn on the River Rhine. (Look for Bonn on the map.)
3. His birthday is December 16, and his birth year was 1770.
4. The Beethoven House is now a Museum.

5. Beethoven's father was a singer.
6. Ludwig began to study music at the age of four.
7. He was shy and quiet in school, always thinking even then of music.
8. Even as a little boy he composed music.
9. When he was ten years old his first published composition appeared.
10. A teacher who helped him very much was Christian Gottlob Neefe.
11. Beethoven learned to play several instruments.

12. He went to Vienna when he was sixteen, met Mozart and had lessons from him.

13. Later, Beethoven met Haydn at Bonn.

14. On Haydn's advice he returned to Vienna, making it his home for the rest of his life.

15. Carl Czerny once called on Beethoven and wrote a fine description of him.

[Pg 14] 16. At about thirty Beethoven became deaf.

17. Most of the great symphonies were composed after he lost his hearing.

18. Beethoven died March 26, 1827, at the age of 57.

SOME QUESTIONS

1. When and where was Beethoven born?
2. Who was his first teacher?
3. What did his father do?
4. How long did little Ludwig go to school?
5. What description of him as a boy in school has been given?
6. How old was he when he first played in public?
7. What composition of his was first to be published?
8. Which of his teachers took great interest in him?
9. What did he say about the little boy's future?

10. Where did Beethoven go when he was sixteen years old?

11. With what two great masters did he study?

12. What composer, as a little boy, went to see Beethoven?

13. How did he describe him?

14. Name some of the forms of music which Beethoven composed.

15. Write a list of music by Beethoven that you have heard.

16. What is a concerto? a sonata?

17. How old was Beethoven when he died?

[Pg 15] THE STORY OF LUDWIG VAN BEETHOVEN

Written by............Tenzin..........
On date............26.8.2016............

Timeless books such as:

FOR KIDS, PARTNERS AND FRIENDS

Alice in Wonderland • The Jungle Book • The Wonderful Wizard of Oz
Peter and Wendy • Robin Hood • The Prince and The Pauper
The Railway Children • Treasure Island • A Christmas Carol

Romeo and Juliet • Dracula

Visit
ImTheStory.com
and order yours today!

he was
honest and
out forte's
was still us?
No we it be
its a my

and it
smelt delgheate

and loves it
died 1827
and born 1747

B

CPSIA information can be obtained at www.ICGtesting.com
Printed in the USA
BVOW02s1902260716

456932BV00029B/270/P